Dr. Zed's Science Surprises

Gordon Penrose

Edited by Janis Nostbakken & Marilyn Baillie

Simon and Schuster Books for Young Readers
Published by Simon & Schuster Inc., New York

SIMON AND SCHUSTER BOOKS FOR YOUNG READERS Simon & Schuster Building, Rockefeller Center, 1230 Avenue of the Americas, New York, New York 10020 Copyright © 1989 by Greey de Pencier Books. All rights reserved including the right of reproduction in whole or in part in any form. Originally published in Canada by Greey de Pencier Books. First U.S. edition 1990. SIMON AND SCHUSTER BOOKS FOR YOUNG READERS is a trademark of Simon & Schuster Inc. Photography by Ray Boudreau, except page 13 by Tony Thomas. Illustrations by Tina Holdcroft, except pages 16 & 17 by Andrew Plewes. Designed by Wycliffe Smith. Manufactured in Hong Kong.

10 9 8 7 6 5 4 3 2 1

10 9 8 7 6 5 4 3 2 (pbk.)

Library of Congress Cataloging-in-Publication Data. Penrose, Gordon. Science surprises / Gordon Penrose ; edited by Janis Nostbakken & Marilyn Baillie. p.   cm. Summary: An illustrated collection of simple and safe science experiments. 1. Scientific recreations—Juvenile literature. 2. Science—Experiments— Juvenile literature. [1. Science—Experiments. 2. Experiments. 3. Scientific recreations.] I. Nostbakken, Janis. II. Baillie, Marilyn. III. Title. Q164.P367 1989 507.8—dc20 89-22012 CIP AC

ISBN 0-671-70542-3 ISBN 0-671-70541-5 (pbk.)

Contents

Egg Games 4

Elec-tricks 6

Presto! Change-o! 8

Secret Messages 10

Body Tricks 12

Taste Test 14

Eye Openers 16

Fingerprints 18

Lost and Found 20

Finger Power 22

Hole in Your Hand 24

High and Dry 26

Card Trick 28

More from Dr. Zed 30

Index 32

Egg Games

Did you know you can remove the shell of an egg without cracking it?

HERE'S HOW:

1. Carefully place an uncooked egg into a glass.

2. Add enough vinegar to cover the egg.

3. Wait for a day. Then gently lift the egg out of the glass. What does it feel like? What happens if you leave the egg covered in the vinegar for three or four days?

Have you ever tried to bounce an egg? Be sure to follow these steps before you do!

1. Place a hard-boiled egg in a glass.

2. Add enough vinegar to cover the egg.

3. After two days, how does the egg feel? Return the egg to the vinegar and wait one more day. Then gently bounce the egg. Try this in the kitchen sink first. How high can you bounce the egg?

That's really egg-citing!

HERE'S AN EGGS-TRA TRICK TO TRY: MAKE AN EGG FLOAT!

Place an uncooked egg in a glass of warm water and gently stir in a few spoonfuls of salt. Watch the egg rise.

Elec-tricks

Your hair will stand on end when you try this trick! It works best on a dry day and with squeaky clean hair.

HERE'S HOW:

1. Rub a blown-up balloon back and forth on your hair.

2. Look into a mirror and slowly pull the balloon away from your head.

3. Watch your hair rise!

4. Now hold the balloon against a wall. When you let it go, does it stick to the wall?

Can a comb pick up paper? Yes!...if it's full of static electricity.

1. Run a plastic comb through your hair several times.

2. Hold the comb near small pieces of tissue paper or bits of paper towel.

3. Watch the paper jump!

Watch the water wiggle!

YOU CAN MAKE WATER WIGGLE WITHOUT EVEN TOUCHING IT.

Turn on a cold water faucet and let the water flow in a slow, steady stream. Then run a plastic comb through your hair. Hold the comb beside the stream of water.
What happens to the water when you move the comb back and forth?

Presto! Change-o!

Make dull pennies dazzle!

HERE'S HOW:

1. Half-fill a glass with vinegar.
2. Drop in old, tarnished pennies and stir.
3. Spoon out the shiny coins. How long do they stay bright?

TRY THE SAME EXPERIMENT AGAIN, BUT WITH A TWIST.

This time add a pinch or two of salt to the vinegar. Does the same thing happen? Then add a heaping spoonful of salt to the vinegar. What happens when these coins are left out to dry?

What a BRIGHT idea!

Secret Messages

Send secret messages to a special friend!

HERE'S HOW:

1. Dip a toothpick or cotton swab in lemon juice and draw or print your message on plain paper.

2. Pour salt on the paper to completely cover the message.

3. When the paper is totally dry, brush away the salt.

4. To see the message, rub a pencil or crayon back and forth across the paper several times.

IF YOU WANT TO READ THIS SECRET MESSAGE FROM DR. ZED, HOLD IT UP TO A MIRROR.

You can use mirror writing to send a secret message of your own. Simply write from right to left across the page, printing the letters of each word backwards.

Body Tricks

Surprise yourself with these body tricks.

HERE'S HOW:

Hop Stopper

1. Bend over and grab your toes.
2. Keep your knees slightly bent.
3. Try to hop forward. Can you hop backward?

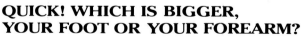

Balancing Act

1. Balance on one foot and count to ten.
2. Have a rest.
3. Balance on one foot again, this time with your eyes closed. What number can you count to before you fall over?

Fool your friends!

QUICK! WHICH IS BIGGER, YOUR FOOT OR YOUR FOREARM?

Find out for sure by measuring your foot from heel to toe with a ruler or measuring tape. Then measure your arm from wrist to elbow. Were you right?

Taste Test

Which would you rather eat, a raw potato or a raw apple? Take a taste test to find out.

HERE'S HOW:

1. Start with peeled slices of uncooked potato and apple.

2. Cover your eyes with a blindfold.

3. Tightly hold your nose with one hand.

4. Take a bite of each slice.
   Can you tell which is which?

TRY THE SAME TEST WITH FRUIT JUICE.

Hold your nose and take a sip of grape juice, then of apple juice. Can you tell them apart?

The nose knows!

Eye Openers

**Can you really believe what you see?
Look carefully at each of these
pictures to find out.**

1 How many faces do you see?

2 Which flower center
is the smallest?

3 How many animals can you find here?

4 Stare at the black squares and count to ten. What else do you see?

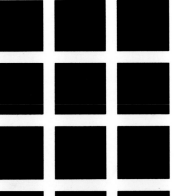

5 Are these stars the same color?

Answers on page 31

Wow! A floating finger!

MAKE YOUR OWN OPTICAL ILLUSION.

Hold your index fingers slightly apart in front of your eyes. Stare at an object beyond your fingers. What do you see floating between your fingers?

17

Fingerprints

**True or false? All members of
your family have the same fingerprints.
Find the answer by collecting and
comparing the fingerprints of your
family and friends. Be sure to wash
your hands before and after
following these steps.**

1 Lightly rub a thin coating of lipstick onto your fingertip.

2 Carefully place your smudged finger on a piece of clear Scotch tape.

3 Peel the tape off your finger and stick it onto a piece of clean paper.

WHICH FINGERPRINT TYPE IS THE MOST COMMON?

**Once you've collected prints of
a number of people, compare
them to each other and to
these fingerprint types.**

Arch

Loop

Whorl

Are you a loop, a whorl or an arch?

Lost and Found

Make a coin disappear right before your very eyes!

HERE'S HOW:

1. Fill a glass with water.

2. Put a coin in the palm of your hand.

3. Place the glass on top of the coin and look down through it to see the coin.

4. Now put your other hand on top of the glass and look for the coin through the side of the glass. Is it still there?

TRY THIS PENCIL TRICK!

Put a pencil in a glass of water and look at it through the side of the glass. What happens to the pencil?

How did it break?

Finger Power

Pick a partner (even one bigger than yourself!) and prove how much power you have in your fingers.

HERE'S HOW:

The Mighty Finger

1. Ask your partner to sit in a straight-backed chair with arms folded, chin up, head high.

2. Press your index finger against your partner's forehead. Can your partner get up out of the chair?

Fighting Fingers

1. Ask your partner to stand with arms fully outstretched and fists pressed firmly together, one on top of the other.

2. Hold out your index fingers and quickly strike them sideways, in opposite directions, against the fists. Can your partner still hold the fists together?

Be a penny pincher!

NOW TEST YOUR FINGER POWER AGAINST A PENNY.

Put your knuckles together. Ask your partner to help you raise your ring fingers and place a penny between them. Here's the challenge: While keeping your knuckles together, can you drop the penny?

Hole in Your Hand

Do you have X-ray vision? Follow these steps to see a hole right through your hand!

1. Roll a piece of paper about twelve inches long into a tube or use an empty paper towel roll.

2. Look straight ahead at some object or spot on the wall.

3. Hold the tube up to one eye so that it completely covers the eye.

4. Hold your other hand, palm open and facing you, halfway along the tube.

5. Keep looking at the object with both eyes.

DID YOU KNOW YOU CAN PUSH A QUARTER THROUGH A HOLE THE SIZE OF A DIME?

Cut a dime-size hole in the center of a piece of paper. Fold the paper in half. Then place a quarter in the center of the fold. Hold the outer edges of the fold, pull upward and wiggle the paper back and forth to ease the quarter through the hole.

Does this make CENTS?

High and Dry

What goes under water but never gets wet? Follow these steps to find the answer.

1 Fill a sink or basin with water.

2 Pack some tissue into the bottom of a drinking glass so that it stays in place when the glass is turned upside down.

3 Hold the glass upside down and push it straight into the water without tipping it.

4 Pull the glass straight up out of the water. Now pull out the tissue. Is it wet or dry? What happens when you tip the glass?

HOW MANY TIMES CAN YOU FOLD A PIECE OF PAPER IN HALF? TWENTY, THIRTY, FORTY TIMES?

Guess again and then try folding paper yourself to see if you are right. Use any kind of paper, from tissue to cardboard.

...5...6 ...7...8 ...?!

26

Card Trick

**With a flick of your finger
you can drop a coin into a glass
without touching it.**

HERE'S HOW:

1. Place a playing card on top of a glass.

2. Put a coin on top of the card.

3. Quickly flick your index finger against the edge of the card. The card flies off, but what happens to the coin?

**YOU CAN DROP A DIME INTO
A SODA POP BOTTLE TOO.**

Balance the coin on top of a strip of paper placed on top of an open bottle. Quickly pull the strip of paper out from under the dime.

More from Dr. Zed

The activities in this book have been carefully selected to give children a "hands-on" introduction to science. In doing these simple experiments, children can make a variety of discoveries that will surprise and delight them. Above all, it is hoped that these activities will encourage children to explore and experiment further, because it is most valuable for them to discover for themselves the many possible outcomes science holds.

There are no "wrong" outcomes to the activities — every finding is valid, and bound to stimulate lots of questions. The following notes suggest explanations and insights into those science concepts that can be discussed simply with young children; questions about more complex concepts are better explored through "hands-on" experimentation than by explanations too abstract for the very young. These notes also include the answers to special challenges scattered throughout the book.

Egg Games
(page 4)
Activity #1

Eggshells contain calcium, so do your bones and teeth. It helps make them strong. Vinegar is an acid which dissolves the calcium in the shell leaving the skin under the shell to hold the egg together. In much the same way as vinegar, acids in your mouth attack your teeth and make holes in them. That's why brushing your teeth is so important.

Activity #3

At first the egg sinks, because it is heavier than water. But when you add salt, the water becomes heavier than the egg, and so the egg floats. This is why it is easier for you to float in saltwater than in freshwater.

Elec-tricks
(page 6)
Activities #1, #2 and #3

The balloon and comb pick up static electricity from your hair. Have you ever felt static electricity when you shuffle across a carpet in stockinged feet?

Presto! Change-o!
(page 8)
Activities #1 and #2

Over time, pennies become dirty. Vinegar is an acid that eats away the dirt to leave the pennies clean and shiny. Salt combines with vinegar to form a stronger acid that works even faster. When the pennies cleaned with salt and vinegar are left out in the air, they turn green. If you don't want your pennies to turn green, wash them with detergent as soon as you take them out of the salt and vinegar mixture, then rinse and dry them.

Secret Messages
(page 11)
Activity #1

When you brush away the salt, you leave a trail of small salt crystals with sharp edges on your message. As you rub the pencil over the paper, more lead catches on the salt crystals than on the rest of the paper. That's why your secret message appears.

Activity #2

You can read the secret message in the mirror because it is written backwards. The mirror flips the printing in the same way that it flips your image when you look in the mirror.

Body Tricks
(page 12)
Activity #2

Eyesight is one of the senses that affects your balance. Standing on one leg unbalances you. Take away your sight, too, and your body cannot stay upright.

Activity #3

Your foot and forearm are exactly the same size! This is true for people of all ages.

Taste Test
(page 15)
Activities #1 and #2

Your tongue can only tell you if food is sweet, sour, salty or bitter. You need your sense of smell to tell one food's flavor from another.

Eye Openers
(pages 16-17)
Activities #1 and #2

Optical illusions can trick your eyes and fool your brain.

Answers to Activity #1

1. There are four faces.
2. All of the flower centers are the same size.
3. There are two animals: a rabbit and a duck.
4. Grey dots appear and disappear.
5. Yes, the stars are the same color.

Fingerprints
(page 18)
Activity #1

No two people in the world have the same fingerprints, not even identical twins. Did you know that no two cats have the same nose prints?

Activity #2

Loops are the most common fingerprint type.

Lost and Found
(page 21)
Activities #1 and #2

Even though water is clear, looking through it changes the way you see things. When you look through the water at an angle, you cannot see the coin. Pour the water out and look through the glass at the same angle. Now you can see the coin. In much the same way, when you look through the water at an angle, the pencil appears to be broken, but if you pour the water out, it looks whole again.

Finger Power
(page 22)
Activity #1
When sitting, all your partner's weight is in his or her seat. To stand up, your partner's head must move forward. Your finger stops the head from moving, the weight from shifting and your partner from standing.

Activity #2
Fingers win over fists every time. Your partner is pressing the fists together in an up-and-down direction. Your fingers attack on the sides.

Activity #3
You cannot drop the penny. If your middle finger cannot move, neither can your ring finger, because the tendons of your middle and ring fingers are joined together.

Hole in Your Hand
(page 24)
Activity #1
You use both your eyes to see an object. Your brain receives a message from each eye and combines them to make the total picture. But in this trick, one eye sees your hand and the other sees the opening through the tube. When these two pictures are combined, you think you see a hole in your hand.

High and Dry
(page 26)
Activity #1
Air gets trapped inside the glass and pushes against the water. The air keeps the water out of the glass and the paper stays dry.

Activity #2
It is impossible to fold any piece of paper in half more than nine times.

Card Trick
(page 29)
Activities #1 and #2
When you flick the card, it moves so quickly that it flies right out from under the coin. The coin drops into the glass. In much the same way, the dime drops into the soda bottle when you quickly pull the strip of paper away.

There's SCIENCE everywhere!

Index

Air: Exerts pressure, 26

Balloon: Charged with static electricity, 6

Body: Balance
affected by eyesight, 12
shift of, affecting center of gravity, 12
Finger on forehead
location of forces, 22
Fingerprint types, 18
Fingers and fists
direction of forces, 22
Fingers trying to drop penny
tendons joined, 22
Floating finger
vision/optical illusion, 17
Foot and forearm
proportions, 12

Hole in hand
vision/optical illusion, 24
Senses, 15

Coins: Cleaning pennies
chemical changes, 8
Disappearing
refraction of light, 21
Dropping
inertia, 29

Comb: Charged with static electricity, 6

Eggs: Removing shell
acids and bases, 4
chemical changes, 4
Density, 4
Floating and sinking, 4

Illusions: Optical, 16-17, 24

Mirrors: Light
reflection, 11
reversing images, 11

Paper: Folding
geometric number/series of folds, 26
Quarter through small hole
elongation by paper flexing, 24

Pencil: In water
refraction of light, 21
Rubbing over salt crystals
friction, 11

Senses: Taste and smell, 15
Vision/optical illusions, 16-17, 24